SPILLING THE CHAI
Poems about Family & Food
GENEFFA JAHAN

Spilling the Chai: Poems about Family and Food
Copyright © Jamii Publishing 2024
Front Cover Design: "Five of Cups" by Geneffa Jahan & Cherie Walkowiak
Back Cover Art: "Eight of Cups" by Geneffa Jahan

ISBN: 978-1-954901-02-5

SPILLING THE CHAI

~Poems about Family & Food~

Geneffa Jahan

For Augie and Maddie who challenge and champion me.
You will inherit, and no doubt perfect the recipes.

In memory of my mother and my masi
who leave me hungry for more.

For our foremothers
who gave us the ingredients,
and for all my relations.

But most of all,
for the women who wonder how much to spill.
I hope this book inspires you to get messy.

NOTES FROM THE KITCHEN

I grew up in a family of split tongues—four of us functioning in two languages. Or was it three? I couldn't know. It was served to me as soup—the diction blended and idioms mixed so that I never knew what I was speaking.

Gujarati was the aggressive tongue my parents reserved for each other. They spoke to us in English, the only language they wanted us to learn—or so I thought. It was at Glastonbury Infants School in Sutton, Surrey, England that I found out otherwise. The sudden confused look from my teachers or peers let me know I had wandered beyond it. But with what? Gujarati? I was to learn that some of our phrases were Swahili—words integrated into my parents' lives growing up in East Africa. To this day, I can't parse the ingredients of some of our common phrases and tell you which words are from which language. It was a tongue authentically ours, but not authentically anything.

Much like the language we used, our food was a hodge-podge of what was available from the grocery shop we lived above— one they ran all day and returned from for dinner, bringing Heinz and Birds Eye to supplement my mother's *chokha* and curry.

She'd start a *vaghar* by frying up a mess of mustard seed and fenugreek with a tin of tomato paste, then add ground coriander, cumin, and turmeric from plastic packages bought at the Indian spice store in London. Occasionally, she'd use cinnamon bark, whole cardamom pods, and twigs of clove. But she used butter instead of ghee. Garlic and ginger came pureed in bottles, though for decades, wherever we lived, my parents grew mint and cilantro and blended our own *lilli* chutney. Mine comes from a bottle I get in Fremont and keep past its expiration in the door of my fridge.

Can we call any of this Indian food? No more than I can claim to speak an Indian tongue. But authenticity means something different to me now. Not how things should be but how they are. Not how we cook for company but how we make do daily. There's a rhythm to these recipes—one might say a poetry.

The earlier poems in this collection capture the magic of making do through the eyes of a child. They reveal the ingredients of my life—one of overlapped languages and bastardized foods—a culinary culture traveling from India to East Africa to England to Canada, and finally, to California. Each poem is a recipe. Together they reveal how the magical thinking of childhood yields to the growing awareness of dysfunction and manipulation—secrets begging to be spilled.

Perhaps my disclosures here can help other readers spill the tea themselves—voicing what must be spoken and seeing with relief that nothing is unspeakable. It was pouring chai on my mother's grave in 2022, as she'd requested or perhaps joked, that the idea for this little book came to me.

So, make yourself a mug of something delicious, pull up a chair, and join me as I spill the chai.

MENU[1]

HIDDEN INGREDIENTS	iii
FIRST COURSE	1
Dizzy Means Banana*	3
Macho Ngombe	5
Kitchree and Cream	7
Barkat	9
Just a Trifle	11
Fists of Flour	13
Nimuk*	15
Cash n' Carry	19
Raining Bacon*	22
Battersea Park	25
Dho Dhokra Daughters	28
Sleeping Seeds	31
SECOND COURSE	33
Lady's Fingers	35
Ralph Klein Samosas	37
Chutney	40
The Side Dish*	43
Fenugreek	44

---

[1] Poems marked by an asterisk (*) depict scenes of physical violence. Reader discretion is advised.

Machi Bhat	46
Kampala Toast	49
Lunching at Lake Louise	50
Chocolate Mints	52
Spoon Mischief	55
Mother Forgets Thanksgiving	57
Buss!	58
Graveside Chai	60
A Personal Glossary	63
Acknowledgements	67
About the Author	69

HIDDEN INGREDIENTS

To be true to the experiences normalized within my family, these poems do not reveal what I was later to learn about my father's mental health struggles. We knew he had survived a traumatic childhood, one he described in great detail, and this is what primarily kept us loyal to him, protective of his behaviors, which he clearly couldn't control.

It was only a couple of years ago that he was given diagnoses that explained his erratic moods, violent rage, and challenges with self-regulation. He was 85, and my mother had already passed away. This book is a testament to the suffering of a man and his family without the resources, tools, and knowledge to address the source of their pain.

After so many decades, it is difficult to disclose the memories that clearly illustrate a family in crisis. I continue to love my father and feel protective of him. I spill the chai not to cause harm but to clear things up. It is well past time to end the taboo of domestic violence and provide compassion for all afflicted on both sides of this dynamic. I wrote this book in hopes that we can start such conversations. As you read, if anything here resonates for you or those you know, please take steps to name and address it now. National and international helplines are included.

Finally, I entrust the reader with gentle handling of the people revealed on the pages that follow. I hope I've been able to show their humor, courage, and resilience as well as their frailties. I suspect this family—my family—is not as unusual as one might think.

National Domestic Violence Hotline (USA):
www.thehotline.org
Call 1-800-799-7233 (24/7) or Text BEGIN to 88788.

MAITRI (San Francisco/Bay Area, California, USA):
www.maitri.org
Call 1-888-862-4874 (Mon – Fri, 9 am – 3 pm)
Maitri is a free, confidential, nonprofit organization based in the San Francisco Bay Area that primarily helps families and individuals from South Asia (Afghanistan, Bangladesh, Bhutan, India, Nepal, Pakistan, Sri Lanka, and the Maldives) facing domestic violence, emotional abuse, cultural alienation, or family conflict (maitri.org).

Monarch Services (Santa Cruz, California, USA):
www.monarchscc.org
Call 1-888-900-4232 (24-hour bilingual crisis line; Linea de crisis disponible 24 horas)

Canadian Association of Social Workers (CASW): https://www.casw-acts.ca/en/resources/family-and-intimate-partner-violence
List of resource agencies addressing Family and Intimate Partner Violence.

National Domestic Abuse Helpline (UK): www.refuge.org.uk
Call 0808-2000-247 (24/7)

FIRST COURSE

Dizzy Means Banana*

To my failing ears, *chakkar* and *chakra* sound the same.
Chakkar the spinning of one's head,
crystals dislodged from the inner ear
throwing the body off-kilter.

Chakra pronounced almost the same,
a spinning of wheels within the body,
a word we understood, could say correctly,
but hardly used, like *Namaste* and *yoga*.

Funny to see that of all the gems to make it out of India,
chakras are still going strong.
Perhaps it's the visual appeal,
seven spinning lotus flowers bright and glowing
strung like Christmas lights up the spine
from root to crown.

But *chakkar* was the word more likely
to surface at home.
My father announcing its arrival
along with a ringing in his ears
and pounding head—
from his *loypirni* wife and daughters
drinking the blood of his patience down to dregs.

I don't remember Mummy saying *chakkar*.
She kept her body's mishaps to herself,
and I used the word dizzy
when I lost balance from
the hand almost larger than my face

though more often than not we didn't use
dizzy that way, learning as girls
to keep the peace with a flexing of the neck,
a spine snapping back into place.

In our house
dizzy meant banana [2]
and I could safely say I didn't want one,
pale and raw, difficult to swallow
the texture of chalk
but easier to reject
than the hand
flying out
to tame my face.

---

[2] Pronounced "dizzy," *ndizi* is the Swahili word for banana. Italicized words are glossed at the end of this book.

Macho Ngombe

We never have eggs for breakfast
when Daddy claims the kitchen

rustling up the eye of a cow
over glistening shards of onion.

The rhythmic beat of his lips and guttural hum
conjure herds he commands in Kiswahili

not my mother's demure *maiyai*.
His cracked eggs descend like a jungle storm

onto a buttered pan
monsoon puddles turning solid

into cattle crying tears of oil
eye to eye with me hungry for breakfast.

How I relish each dish, each name
and how he conjures one into the other

each fried egg, a safari
safe in Surrey but ready to fill me

with the Africa cooked up in Daddy's stories.
His talent to transmogrify

knows no restriction.
His words can be lard or halal

for daughters devouring translations
we tuck into daily.

Daddy feeds us a world where Indians worship cows
and Africans eat their eyes.

In Daddy's world
we can do both.

Kitchree and Cream

                I want Mummy
              Mummy is in hospital.
            Then I want kitchree

                I want Mummy
           Mummy is in too much pain.
       Then I want butter in my kitchree

                I want Mummy
    Mummy is with the crying baby—listen!
       Then I want cream on my kitchree

                            I stare at the mound
                            of rice and mung
                            packed tight with butter
                            under a dripping cap
                            of Devon double cream
                            spilling into rivulets
                            that gather in a moat
                            around the base

I am not yet three
but I know if I throw myself atop
I will slide down just the same
seeping into the cracks
I find here and there

                            Mostly
                            I will melt
                            into the moat
                                          the mound
                                          no longer
                                          meant
                                          for me

Barkat

She was not a woman of precise measurements
but of *utker*
hands flying from bottle to bottle
Lazy Susan spinning
pressure cooker hissing
dish towels hanging askew with her handprint
tinged yellow from *hardar* and flecks of cilantro

Craning my neck
my eyes
could barely keep up with this
well-rehearsed dance
pots taking turns on the only working burner
feet ready to pivot
hands leading the way

Once eye level with the counter
I wanted to know how much.
How will I learn these recipes?

Just watch, she'd say:
       a pinch of mustard seed
       a handful of *methi* flakes
       a scoop of *dhana jeera*
Everything measured by hand and learned by heart

Once the curry was ready
she'd add a few strands of saffron
       then another

Lifting the lid to release steam
she'd add a *teepu* of cream
       then another

for *Barkat*, she'd say
        with every extra drop
for *Barkat*, she'd say
        with each over-priced saffron strand
for *Barkat*, she'd say
        with each frivolous cardamom pod

Barkat was a metric she could teach:
        Cook as if each meal is for *mehman*
        always giving more than what is asked.
        That is how the food will show our love

Just a Trifle

"It's nothing special," she insists,
and hoists the crystal bowl larger than a placemat
onto the counter where packages from Cash n' Carry
gather to watch.

"What is it, then?" I ask
as she slices even rounds of jelly roll,
lays them flat in a circle inside the bowl
curlicues of jam oozing from vanilla cake
waiting for custard.

"It's just a trifle," she says
smoothing a layer of custard to conceal
the carefully placed, sliced rounds of roll.

"A silly pudding," she adds
pouring in syrupy tangerine wedges
covered with another layer of custard,
ashamed that they're not strawberries
any more than we're English.

"It won't show and will taste just as yum"
she declares as she lays down
a blanket of freshly whipped cream,
a snowscape she smooths with the
back and forth glide of a spatula
waved like a wand to obscure the careful work below.

Eye-level with the sides of the bowl I can see
the layers of her labor
in stripes of orange wedge and amber sponge,
the smoothness of custard,
the topcoat of cream with concentric circles
of grapes, red and green, and pineapple chunks.

I know how it will go
once my mum removes her apron,
smooths back her hair
greets our guests,
lays out crustless sandwiches
of cucumber and watercress,
around the trifle centerpiece.

"This looks lovely," they will say.
"You shouldn't have," some will add.
"Oh, it's nothing," she will lie.
And I'll watch and learn how
the work of a woman is to disappear.

Fists of Flour

The only time I saw her
make a fist
was with flour

She was soft like that
and like flour
the more I squeezed
the less of her
there was.

I watched her work
the underside of knuckle
and all the nameless veins
that went into the making of *muthia*
a dumpling called fist for its final shape
and pattern of sunken relief.

Counter-high, I'd watch her pour water
subdue a mountain of mingled flours
semolina, chickpea, pearl millet
a blanket of spices folded in
enthralled by her kneading hands.

She'd tear off a handful and squeeze it
tight enough to turn her knuckles white
drop it in a pan of heating oil
bits of dough clinging to her fingers
till she floured them off
to stir the adjacent pot of curry
then drop the dumplings in.

Sitting down to dinner
I could see the mark
of her fist upon the meal
the imprint of clenched needs
in the grooves and trenches of
the cooked dough.

I would eat around the floating fists
take my time with the vegetables and *russ*
then say I wasn't hungry anymore.

I couldn't explain
why my throat refused to swallow

a meal of drowning women
fists raised high in
a pockmarked stew

dumplings
that taste
of despair

Nimuk*

            1.

(England 1973)

She worried at first she'd forgotten the *nimuk*
but now she knew it was worse than that

knew it as soon as she saw the metal spoon
with its telltale crystal coating
at the bottom of the kitchen sink.

But hadn't she just wiped the same spoon
carelessly with the hem of her blouse

just those few lingering grains
the spoon mostly clean
cloudy from constant wash and wear?

She'd set it down on the lime vinyl counter
to use again only

to see its twin in the sink
and now she knew
it could mean just one thing:

Two scoops of salt in the *kadhi*
Two scoops of salt

overpowering the fragrant yogurt blend
the dash of lemon and
surely he would notice but when?

And how heavy the ladle
And how hot the turmeric-tinged soup

And which direction
or whose
would he throw it?

2.

    thunk
        STOP!
    thunk
        CRYING!
    thunk
        STUPID!
    thunk
        GIRL!
taste ash
and salt
seeping into
mouth in thin line
from throat
lights go off and on
then off/on, offon, offonoffonoffon
too fast
loud sounds of
anger no longer
making words
she braces herself
for the lag
between crunch of skull
against wall and
swing of soft thing inside
delayed by its heft
a wrecking ball to ricochet
against the back of her head
the wall within
that moment's shudder
between first and second thud

is what she learns
to dread most
the first thud only hurts
the second makes
eyes water
teeth rattle
ears pound
nose run
legs swaying useless in air
shoulders held tight
in Daddy's hands

    3.

(California 2023)

Now I can't find *nimuk* anywhere.
Namak I am told is the word in Hindi,
so why did my parents exchange the "a" for an "i"?

Even more bemusing
is the Gujarati word for salt,
mithum, so close to their nickname for me.

They told me Mithu meant Sweetie,
the only thing they called me.
Were they mistaken?

    4.

I'd been looking for *nimuk*
when it turned up on my brain scan
50 years after the fact

tiny, calcified specks
the doctor described then displayed
hyper-intensities scattered at random

like grains of rice
spilled from a burlap sack
grains of salt hardened on a stainless-steel spoon.

                    5.

I'm more than just my Basmati brain.
Maybe *I* am the *nimuk* I've been looking for
the grain with which we're told to take all things

Perhaps I've found the salt
my ancestors marched for
the salt for which I was flung

from which I fled
for which even now
I pay

Cash n' Carry

There is nothing more depressing than a wheel
of cake melting under a cellophane tent in a window box
and two girls under seven buckled within reach.

We take turns playing *Simon Says* and *I Spy* trying not to gape
at the rings of fruit glistening in the late orange sun
the melting cream dripping down the smooth golden sponge.

When a perfectly frosted trapezoid of dried pineapple picks up
speed and slips over the edge, I stop mid-Simon to say,
"Quick!" and tear open the box, dive for the falling fruit.

It's a hand-to-mouth rescue, some from the gold tray crimped
like a cloud at the base of the box, other pieces of candied
ginger and orange wedges captured in mid-fall until the outer
ring is gone.

The concentric circles of fruit that remain break the pattern
so we decide to demolish the ring second from the edge.
And so we proceed until the surface is laid bare,
the pockmarked evidence of our crime.

* * *

There is nothing more deceptive than a circle
whether a cake with too many layers or a *jalebi*'s spiral of sugar.
Mummy says "We'll make one more round" as she buckles us in
to wait.

The sun drips colors down the sky and still we sit
like the good girls we'd been inside Cash 'n Carry, riding on the
dolly, singing jingles with Daddy: "Maybe we'll P-P-Pick Up a
Penguin," he joked as we looked for my birthday cake.

"All because the lady loves Milk Tray," I retorted pointing to the chocolate.
"Cadbury made us and they covered us in chocolate,"[3]
Daddy clowned a diversion and decided on the prettiest specimen—white with glazed fruit encircling the dome.

We were still singing jingles back and forth, two girls on a dolly with a cake when a man sauntered up, "Oi—Paki—not here!"
We didn't understand.
"No children inside," he added firmly, ignoring the sounds of girls and boys around us.

"Of course, Sir!" Daddy responded, and they rushed to buy the cake, return it to the car where the girls could sit and guard it, and they could shop for their business undisturbed.
Rounds later, they return in the dimming light to see we have guarded the cake too well.

* * *

There is nothing more oppressive than a pattern
allowed to continue. They pause for a moment in shock. Their disbelief more painful than a slap. "We'll take it back!" they exclaim almost in unison. "Say it's defective!"

I know how this will go. If all goes well, they will return with a new wheel of cake.
If not, we will drive home in silence, my parents slightly deflated that they lost.
Either way, I will have had my cake.

---

[3] "P-p-p pick up a penguin," "All because the lady loves Milk Tray," and "Cadbury makes them and they cover them in chocolate," were jingles accompanying adverts in the UK during the 1970s and early '80s. The last of these was a variation on the melody of "Banana Boat (Day-O)."

They don't know it's my thumb that pokes through the thin foil cap of the milk bottles delivered each morning.
The ones they send back as spoiled. I have learned to drink a little from the top of each one.

Getting my fill of cream, I feel a little less robbed of my due, a little more rascal and less Mithu as I'm learning how naughty can feel nice. How heavy can be light. How the cream you expect to sink will somehow manage to rise.

Raining Bacon*

Weebles wobble but they don't fall down.[4]

There are no Weebles in this poem.
Just a mother on a ladder
half-way up
and a child on the ground
empty fists squeezed in on themselves
watching the man's hands and voice rise
as he hurls obscenities at the
woman
Rand sahlee, Junglee sahlee
and bacon
whole packs of it
aimed at her head.

As Muslims, we dodge bacon.
As *weparis*, we don't mind selling it

though it's a Friday.
Mummy in her favorite *khane* frock
that swishes around her ankles
has stocked the tins for Saturday so we can
make the long drive to Putney without
Daddy complaining of too much to do
when we get back.

But she forgot the bacon
and says over her shoulder she will get it later.
He doesn't like the way she says it
dismissively, like making the first prayers in time

---

[4] Weebles were an egg-shaped toy first launched by Hasbro in the US and Airfix in the Uk in the 1970s. The jingle was coined by advertising executive, J. Mitchell Reed (Ward, Arthur. *The Other Side of Airfix*, Pen and Sword 2013).

is more important than making money.

That's how Daddy takes it.
Don't take it that way! Mummy cajoles.
Don't take it that way! I silently plead.
But he takes it that way
takes the box of bacon and throws it down
where thin plastic packs of it slither out like fish.

Mummy scrambles up the ladder.
I hide under the cheese counter
see the hem of her dress swish around her ankles
as she wobbles there in sandals.

Why has she climbed the ladder without the bacon?
Is she lazy? Daddy gathers the packs in a bundle.

The word for throw is *feck*
and as he throws he taunts,
"You want me not to feck?"
"You want me not to feck?"

With one hand on the ladder
Mummy tries with the other
to catch the bacon packets
sailing past her.

I watch one bounce off her face
American-style streaky bacon
rashers carefully arranged in pink shingles,
the slabs evenly layered
like thin white marble steps or
the painstaking pleats of a sari,
pressed within packs that could be pretty if
they'd not become bullets.

The ladder wobbles. Mummy wobbles.

I whisper a chant through my cage of white bars made of teeth
Be a Weeble, Mummy, be a Weeble!

It is raining bacon, but this is all wrong.
The bacon is raining up.
Mummy is falling down.

>By now we have missed first *Dua*.
>There will be no *khane* tonight
>no *ginan*, *farman*, or upstanding
>*tasbih*, second *Dua* or *niyaz*:
>Friday rituals that bring
>boredom and comfort.
>
>I see glimpses of Mummy
>squirming on the ground
>disentangling from fabric
>as Daddy kicks her to get up.
>*Gadheri, there is work to do.*
>
>She mounts the ladder again
>this time with the bacon
>squeezed under both armpits
>one plastic pack between her lips.
>Both hands clutching
>the sides of the ladder
>she hoists herself
>up rung by rung
>
>And without
>dropping a single one
>she lines the packets up
>behind the chilled window
>tenderly leaning
>one against the other
>so they don't fall down.

Battersea Park

Battersea Park has a fun fair.
We've been there before
to ride the boats
that swing into the sky
and fling back from the sun

waited in line to squish our small girl bodies
into cars that collide
or get stuck in a jam
and only go one direction

we've ridden the roundabout dozens of times
and octopus arms that make your stomach churn
your throat convulse
enough to spill.

But the challenge is managing spills along the way,
our Volvo weaving in and out of traffic

                                              Mummy crying
                                            Baapre, the boot!

Daddy's temper flaring with every wrong turn
till Mummy stops pestering

                                    Will we make it in time?
                                    Will it have gone cold?

And then the tires hit gravel and we've parked.
Mummy opens the boot
lifts the *suferiya* lid to behold
what we came for

Chana Bateta—mostly intact
potatoes a bit mushy
still firm at the center
chickpeas split open
splayed flat around the edges of the saucepan
like amber leaves wet against the autumn pavement.

On camp chairs that barely hold
our swaying bottoms
we sit in the parking lot
facing each other

Daddy remembers Africa
how everything tastes better in a tiffin
and Mummy agrees

Battersea Park has a fun fair. We've done this before.
Our meal marked by the sun dripping gold
into the rocking boats, bumping cars, flying swings.

We will eventually go inside and be thrown about
tossed, bumped, and dropped.

We will wait too long in line to be disappointed
by the roundabout of horses.
Sick from watching them go up and down in circles
we will choose a chariot that stays put

and Daddy will complain about not getting
our money's worth because he paid
for us to go up and down
not just round and round.

But no disappointment can touch this—
the magic moment between arrival and entrance
the foamy warmth, tangy tomato
familiar on my tongue

Daddy's eyes shining
and Mummy's best smile,
the *suferiya* not quite empty

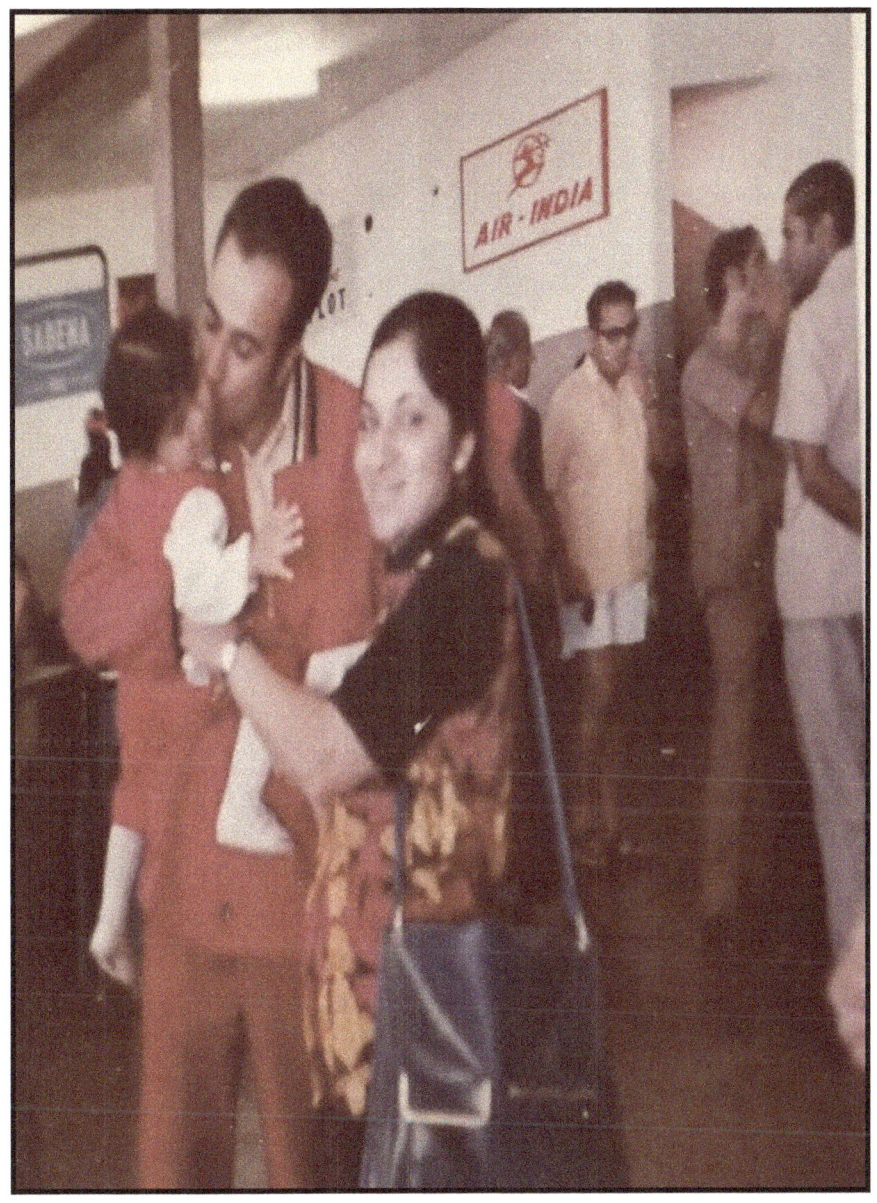

Dho Dhokra Daughters

Dho dhokra ni dikree!
We understood long before
we knew what it meant:
daughters worthless as two *dhokras*
sold on the side of the street in Tanzania
or maybe Mumbai. A snack
called *nasta* when paired with chai
or sometimes the cuter *kuttuck-buttuck*
but delivered by Daddy as a rebuke alongside
his only touch, a *tamacho*.

Not duh but duh!
Daddy's outrage paired with disbelief
I'd not learned to grasp
the nuance of his tongue—
not hitting the upper palate
but flattened against
the upper teeth so one can see
a sliver of tongue striking
the white enamel bars
the only thing holding back
its serpentine reach.

                          My tongue is just too long
                          for this linguistic yoga
                          the teeth too crowded
                          the lower jaw inadequately
                          formed, a blocked nose,
                          a lack of pillow
                          a mouth breather by night
                          and by day taking in
                          the world unfiltered
                          a straight shot to the lungs.

> My tongue bears the engravings
> of toothmarks my dentist shows me
> in a mirror that displays
> the nightly battle not to bite my
> tongue.
> There's not enough room
> and nothing to be done
> "unless we pull 'em all out"
> which I think about although I
> know he jests.
>
> I have learned to cope with my
> mouth a cramped cave
> a wash of fluid always flowing
> down the back wall.

As a child, I hadn't known what to do
with all the water in my mouth.
Afraid to swallow
spitting all day into a tissue
Mummy called "yacky"
her word for when yuck made her mouth open wider
to make more room for disgust.

As a child, I didn't know
which words they made up
and which ones they borrowed
to make do between tongues.

I couldn't ask about the words I couldn't say
like *dho*, which I understood as two
even though the word is "*beh*" in Gujarati.

And why not a more conjugated snack?
Was *dhokra* the best that he could do?
I've learned to make it finally with ease
sliced up into a dozen diamond squares

a savory sponge, tinted yellow from turmeric
dainty but for the tangy lemon leaves
and black mustard seeds dancing on top.

The type of flour doesn't matter
—chickpea or semolina—
but it must contain Eno,
a secret ingredient
from the pharmacy aisle.

In *dhokra* and in daughters
acid and liquid combine
into the byproduct of breath
pushing its way to the dome
of whatever traps it there.

The remedy we use
to keep our hearts from burning
makes *dhokra* light and fluffy
makes daughters steam and rise.

Sleeping Seeds

Soowa means to sleep. *Dhana* is seed
Soowadhana—the more elegant name
for the dinner's parting gesture
the host's farewell

the other being *mukhwas*, "mouth stench"
as if the meal had run out of metaphor

at that late hour, all eloquence consigned
to ornate silver dishes, dainty embellished
spoons swirling mountains of color
into a kaleidoscope of pulse and pearl

the flattened teardrop of fennel
clear quartz of crystalline sugar
and tiny egg-shaped sweets of impossible pink
with a splinter of mint.

When it was time to make the rounds
I clamored to be chosen to circle the room
and drop a few seeds in the sea of cupped hands
raised as if in prayer, an inverted grace lifted
not to Allah but an over-zealous girl

I would tip the seeds from spoon
to hands soft, supplicant, ready to receive
my shower of blessings
a thimble's worth of *baksheesh* for each one.

Like a palmist, I would study
the underside of bone
plump pillows of flesh
seeds stuck in crevices
the children could lick off their hands

But adults would cup
the tiny mound to their lips
and with a sudden jerk
toss their heads back
like horses now

free, unfettered
heads taking turns
to snap back and take my seeds
a sudden flash of throat
before they disappeared
wound beneath scarves
or tucked under *toppees*
seeds gathered, dispersed, driven home.

I wondered then if it was really
the seeds that were sleeping
or the *saga*

their word for story
our word
for people who share your line

but now I know
that all of us were sleeping
all of us, seeds, saga

stories
waiting to be roused

by a new dawn
or the next day's meal

SECOND COURSE

Lady's Fingers

In England I was too young
to be trusted with a knife.
I watched as Mummy slit the lady's fingers
clean white seeds stained with masala
she stuffed in every crevice
before swiping them into the red-hot oil
to simmer and stew.

When we had English company one night
Daddy told us not to call it *bhindi*
hoping to impress them with its English name:
Lady's Fingers for the dainty shape
he proudly reported
but I couldn't see it then and didn't believe him
like our guests who exchanged glances
and dove for the potatoes.

I felt bad Mummy's fingers had been wasted
and brought myself to eat a few.
Eventually, I learned to like the taste
even crave it.

* * *

In Canada each winter I observe
her fingers slit from the cold
retracted cuticles peeled back
revealing crevices that bleed pink
onto the shovel she hoists to
clear a path through the snow.

She seldom has time to cook
so I learn to heat boil-in-the-bag
dinners of Salisbury steak or Monterey Chicken.

Gone is the slender elegance of *bhindi*
the shapely knuckles and tapered fingers
slit gently and stuffed with dry spices.

Now we split open our swollen bags of salty meat and gravy
take our plates to gather in the front room
to watch pre-taped shows of Oprah
and Jeopardy.

Ralph Klein Samosas

        1.

Hullo, chullo!
Jaldi! We will be late
for the ribbon-cutting ceremony

Hullo, chullo!
Jaldi! We will be late
for the cake-cutting ceremony

Hullo, chullo!
Jaldi! We don't want to miss it—
Ralph Klein is going to eat a samosa!

Invite your non-Ismaili friends and we will smash them all inside the car like bhajia
and take them to Max Bell Arena!

Daddy must be joking
I don't have that many friends.

        2.

I don't know how to explain *Kushiali*
or the orange stain of *mehndi* on my hands

how we adore our *Imam*
his birthday revered, his coronation honored every year
yet it's the mayor of Calgary who quickens us now.

My friends are not impressed that he will be there.
Yes—he had gone to our high school
but so had Tommy Chong
both of them dropouts at 16.

How could they understand
we haven't come for a cake or a crowning
or even for *dandiya raas.*

We have parked, shuttled, and walked
to feed a white man a samosa
an Englishman. . . Canadian yes, but English
as we call all those considered White.

Not the kind of English in Africa
who threw parties my parents could only gape at from afar

Nor the prior colonials who cast Indians across seas
to do their bidding on another continent

But the kind who meets us where we are
extends his welcome
curries our vote.

               3.

Show me a white man who means his Mubarak
and I'll show you a Ralph!

He opens wide
tips back his head
angles half the wedge
into his mouth
then chomps down
ingredients spilling past his lips
a strand of cabbage
dripping yellow oil
left to dangle from his chin.

"Clap! Everybody, clap!"
The *mukhi* can hardly contain
his enthusiasm turning between
throngs of watchers
and Ralph Klein's overstuffed face.

We clap wildly
thousands of hands in concert as if
beating out a percussive prayer.

We don't need ribbons
or cakes
we don't need
crowns
we just need
a white man willing
to take a bite
from a triangle
we've all been fed.

Chutney

"Gujarati lili chatni is a beautiful thing. As green as the greenest grass, it is a shiny, sparkling emerald pool, spicy, satisfying, and versatile" (Anala.co.uk).

What pound of flesh exacted in the day
made Daddy demand
his evening soup be red?

"*Laal!*" he'd rage at my mother's
brown concoction bubbling on the stove
with big bones from the butchers

meaty bones they were called
to my puzzlement
unwrapping the hollow sanded

rings with no marrow within
or meat without
popped in to float and make the soup a stew.

Daddy didn't mind the empty bones
floating like mood rings in the broth
its color—a measure of his control.

We couldn't move on to another meal
until she got the soup right
so I pulled out a mental color wheel.

Equal parts desperate and curious
we doubled the beefsteak tomatoes
and cans of tomato paste

but once in the stew I saw their hue
muddled by mint and cilantro
Lili chutney blended and bottled from our backyard.

Just don't add chutney! No one adds chutney to soup!
I'd found the solution to stanch his rage
but Mummy would not hear it.

Let him explode! Her chin set. The chutney stayed
snaking through bone rings and carrots like algae,
an alchemy of plant and sea.

My mother couldn't control the soup
but she could trust the garden
to calm not his nerves but her own.

I'm left to wonder,
what shared plans did they bury in the cracked
Calgary soil, that strip of brown in front of the garage?

Did their hands mingle, tips sometimes touching
barely there moments of intimacy
the way they sowed children?

Was it the way his excitement flared when
he brought her the leaves, etched and smooth
distinct yet tangled, ready for her to blend

a smooth consistency
greener than grass
pleasing them both for a moment?

The Side Dish* [5]

She doesn't know how to say sorry
in her father's language,
but she can now say cucumber.

Kah-kree! He spits,
punctuating the word with a whack upon her head,
this spindly English-garden variety green—a side dish—
suddenly central to his point.

Kahkree! A pendulum dashing against one cheek
then swinging to the other,
so she can all the time remember
he doesn't want zucchini in his *raita* even though
the *Cooking Indian Yourself* recipe lists it as an option.

The produce matters as much as anything.
If there's not a Gujarati word for it, it just won't do.
Not in her father's *raita*. Not in the world of his language
where long green vegetables serve many purposes
before they reach the plate,
and most meals are eaten in silence.

---

[5] Unlike the other poems, the details here are not drawn from a specific memory. Rather, the poem displays the kinds of irritants that would provoke my father's rage and its expression. A version of this poem from the first-person perspective was published in the *Porter Gulch Review*. I have switched this version to the third-person perspective to differentiate it from the other poems, drawn from personal experience and direct memory.

Fenugreek

I've used fenugreek
only a handful of times in my life—
each time finding fresh satisfaction
in the way it makes me gather, purse,
and spread my lips in the saying,
each time wondering why
I haven't used fenugreek
more often.

Fenugreek brings to mind my *masi*
though she wanted me to use her given name,
a privilege for me and just one cousin.
During our cooking sessions between my degrees,
she showed me how to scoop a cup of seeds
first swirling out debris with a finger.
Swinging her handful of seeds up
to make a "c" that starts from the bottom,
she would let them spill into sizzling oil
already fragrant with garlic and ginger.
Fenu*greek*? She would lift the end of the word as a question,
unsure of the correct word in English but trying just the same.

Cooking together, we never used fenugreek alone,
not the word nor the spice.
Methi always followed *rai*,
the mustard seed first and foremost
with flecks of fenugreek mixed in to make a *vaghar*,
and from there we'd build a curry.

Years later, shortly before she died
we cooked together one last time, and she said,
"Let's start the *vaghar*, reaching for the *rai methi* blend,"
while I grabbed the individual spices off the merry-go-round
rack

and we laughed because it takes more time to add them separately,
and she didn't see the point
the way I did.

I wanted to contemplate each spice, singular and subtle before it joined the mix.
I wanted to speak in a language where we could be our distinct selves, one at a time.
I yearned for separation then.

That was a century past.
Now I look for the ready-made blend of *rai methi*
and smile to think of Guli, my Masi,
holding court in the kitchen,
hungry for the time we spent together.

Machi Bhat

1.

Her diagnosis came at the end of a full-course meal
old-style *machi bhat*, curried chunks of fish
with spiced rice

slow cooked together for hours, to cultivate the flavor of festival
meals. Guli fussing it was local ling cod and not
the tilapia of her youth.

With at least 20 people in her condo, she laid down
freshly pressed sheets with place settings
and tumblers of *chash*.

She had me count and lay out the special silverware
and Cousin water down the front walk so no footfall would grind
against dirt or track it in.

A hand pressed to her belly from time to time, face pale,
we pushed her to take things slow.
Cousin suggested a medical visit but she said No.

It was just the mayhem, the meal, the hours sprinkling and
ironing bedsheet-tablecloths and linen napkins that drained the
blood from her face.

I understand now it wasn't denial but respect
for the menu of life, items lived in order with as much spice
as fate would allow.

2.

For years I thought Guli was the heart and mind of the clan, but now I see she was its guts and lungs

the lesson of her life, how to expand and contract to fully fit its contours end-to-end

even as it closed in with coups and new continents she nursed a talent for keeping both appetite and dignity intact:

cutting the fur coat donated by the Red Cross in Montreal to fall fashionably to the knee though her shins were punished by the next day's snow

sleeping in paper curlers once relocated to Winnipeg, wanting to look stylish and grateful for her factory job assembling bellbottom jeans

yet walking to save bus fare to and from her teaching job in Richmond, BC, nickels saved to give her father and his wife when they could be found and sent.

All of it a carefully calculated contraction and expansion of which she was author, breather and bellows, humble and proud.

Accepting chemotherapy but putting equal hope in the special black tea to be kept out of the light, she was angry when I opened the fridge

cried "I'm not ready to die!" She'd applied to do a Master's, volunteer in Pakistan, but weeks after feeding us *machi bhat*, she locked up and moved in with her brother.

3.

Gulshan means garden, and for most of her days she cultivated Fragrant Clouds
bouquets of roses to take to *jamatkhana*, but really, she was all about flavor.

When her clothes were divided and I got my share, I shut them away tightly in a trunk to open at times and savor her smell

of food not flowers, faint now
but the memory of flavor remains.

GULSHAN RAJABALI AHMED
(1937 - 1995)

Kampala Toast

My people's legacy lies less in our stories than our recipes,
a way not to remember or retrace
but to repeat

a waft of *agarbatti*, a *Bismillah* before meals,
Guli lived these rituals daily
and ended each night with *Khuda Hafiz*

but in her final weeks
it was recipes she wanted to outlive her—
the making of a thing just so.

A mound of tumored flesh beneath the covers
her strong nasal tone still full of purpose
she told us how to make Kampala toast

made fresh daily at their Diamond Bakery
and Crested Crane restaurant on Kampala Road—
both seized during the coup.

We'd heard the stories before but now
needed to know the making of the thing itself,
the importance of caraway seed, the right amount of oil.

That recipe would be her last dictation
but I recall a final request
once she slipped into a steady sleep

delirium setting in, she awakened once
to ask with great politeness
if they could add just a little more

black pepper to her IV,
still thinking of all sustenance as soup,
and wanting us to get the flavor right.

Lunching at Lake Louise

We don't want to block the view!
Mum tells my brow-raised husband fairly new
to our family and its way of picnics.

I've flounced down our blanket on the rocks
the ones resembling finely polished stones
not quite touching the water's edge.

It's that spot we all know, facing the three,
the snow-patched Mt. Victoria flanked by the rugged peaks of
Niblock and Whyte a stubble of spruce thickest at the base.

Tourists snap pictures, but we sit facing each other
two and two, three of us elated to be four again
now that my American spouse is with us.

Unsure of whether to take in the view or mirror us,
he sits at a slant, each of us on a corner
of the waterproof, fleece-lined sheet.

My mother concentrates on the crockery
unpacking the Tupperware holding our *bateta champ*
covered in napkins soggy from condensation.

I'd begged her to make *bateta champ* for this trip not the easier
bateta wara with ground meat and potatoes fried together
but the delicately filled potato shells.

I'd imagined us circling the lake, our lunch in tow,
taking bites as we dipped our toes in the blue-green lake,
perching a moment to finish a mouthful before we went on.

I'd forgotten she'd bring chutney! Ceramic plates,
scalloped ivory rimmed with pink roses
and ribbed ramekins to hold our condiments.

People regard us from afar as they dig into bags of chips
they share, crumbs falling on rocks,
a soda in the crook of an elbow.

But that is not our way. We are always immigrants
in a place of beauty—come to match
the landscape, not stand out.

Seated on fabric of cerulean blue
my mother has spread out the plates
like points on a star

around the centerpiece of stuffed potato orbs.
Sister has folded patterned napkins into triangles
she's laid beside each plate.

I laugh and exchange glances with my spouse
at my mother's concern that we might
block the view.

Did she not know how physics tricks the eye—
how we were barely visible to those behind us
gazing at the mountain peaks?

But remembering back, I see her real intent.
Her careful work to complement the scene,
to celebrate the symmetry we'd found.

Chocolate Mints

I gassed up my car after hugging my husband
longer than we'd ever hugged before
and he said, "You should get gas,"
so I did at AJ's, just across the street.

Both back at the condo,
we didn't talk about the news.
He'd already turned it off
and I'd seen what I needed
on my work computer before
we were all sent home.

We each started making calls to loved ones,
but when I called my mum and sis in Canada,
to say, "We're okay," they said, "Why wouldn't you be?
You're not in New York or DC."

"But listen,
we were hoping you could send us chocolate mints—
the kind you can get at Trader Joe's."

So the days after 9/11
in my gassed-up car, I went on a quest
for chocolate mints because I thought
it would be easier than
trying to explain how
I didn't want to leave the house
didn't feel safe in my skin, on the streets, or even online.

We'd not yet had a pandemic, so this was the closest I'd
yet lived to a panic of people filling their carts with toilet
paper, canned goods, and water. And little plastic flags.

American flags on the rear of cars, then store windows,
doors and lapels. And in that din,
I asked for chocolate mints.
I had to describe them, the brand,
the size of the tin,
why I need to mail them to Canada
where they don't have this kind of thing.

"You mean, Chocolate mints?" the girl at Trader Joe's
asked without irony.
Then, "Sorry, we don't have them anymore."

"Chocolate mints?" The man at the corner market thought
he heard me wrong,
then said, "No Ma'am," and briskly walked away.

I clearly felt ashamed and frivolous,
yet I continued on this fruitless quest.

I think I know the reason I kept looking
and using up my gas driving around.

It gave me something definite to chase—
a name, a label, a paradox of flavors that had lived

in a box of mints my sister had enjoyed
and in her innocence asked for again

just like I want to ask again for things
that once were so much easier to find

calmness at airports
safety at mosques
flags that don't feel like rebukes

the paradox of a chocolate mint
sweet and sharp
each flavor balancing
the excess of the other
like we used to do as people.

Spoon Mischief

The day I could no longer fit inside my family
I pulled out my nest of measuring spoons

marveled how they stayed attached
on a steel ring to be spread apart

scooping and pouring,
a spoonful of cumin, a tablespoon of turmeric

each bowl extended and filled to its distinct capacity,
but able in an instant to snap back into its nest.

I wondered at the mechanics of it all,
pondered how each curved scoop

with its uniquely colored depression
was somehow perfectly designed

to fit inside the next in size with a flick
of the wrist at the recipe's completion.

I pulled out the recipe for *cobby no saag*
written decades ago in my mother's hand

noticed how she indicated teaspoon with a lower-case "t,"
but tablespoon with a capital.

I remembered that the Gujarati word for teaspoon
chumchi, takes the feminine form

while the word for tablespoon, *chumcho*
takes the masculine

but the idiom *chumcha-giri*

> **spoon mischief**: when someone butters you up then stabs you in the back

takes the generic, neutral form

the language understanding better than I
that size and gender are no metrics for betrayal.

For though I used my nest of spoons in good faith that
day, *Dhana* and *jeera* spilling with deft precision
I couldn't help but notice that a heaped *chumchi*
and a level *chumcho*

deliver the same
serving of spice.

Mother Forgets Thanksgiving

Mother watches the turkey
beady black eyes darting side to side

The turkey is being cooked by Rachel Ray.
Mother watches Rachel Ray cook the turkey

Neck extended, creped like an accordion
breast heaving and shuddering between breaths.

What does she think she's doing? Mother asks
my sister in something between disgust and distress.

*Mummy, it's Rachel Ray! The cooking show you always like
to watch. She's cooking a turkey for Thanksgiving,
Mummy, tomorrow.*

Mother looks confused. *Cooking the turkey?*
Yes, Mummy—you've cooked so many turkeys before!

My sister recounting the story hesitates now,
the phone goes dead for a moment but then she adds,

Mother had asked, *but doesn't it hurt the turkey?*
Is the turkey still alive? Is it in pain?

I want to know the same
and if there's pain.

Buss!

Buss is our word for "that's enough!"
A word to stay the zealous host's ladle
A word to stop the jealous lover's rifle

playfully uttered or shrieked as a warning
a word as clear as a gesture
sound as a gong

calling us to dinner
it should have bothered me all those years
Daddy said *buss* and Mummy kept on serving

and once my uncle got a scalded hand
placed over his cup as he said *buss* to more chai
but Mummy not quite listening kept pouring.

Years later after family intervention
when Uncle and Sister brought them to the table
to encourage divorce

I heard she kept on offering more chai
while he raged that she'd been talking of his temper
to others who were telling her to leave.

She told him to cool it with a saucer she handed him
and biscuits for dipping, disappearing to refill the teapot
returning to her seat from time to time

as if the conversation didn't concern her
not knowing how to face him with her *"Buss!"*
Always the one to offer not decline.

If I'd not been away at university
my *buss* would have been there loud and clear
my fist slamming the table, spilling chai.

Instead, they played that game until she died.

Graveside Chai

The

chai

went

sideways

carried

by

the

wind

Droplets

the

color

of

her

skin

Pictured: Geneffa Jahan & Madeline Aliah
Photo Credit: August Jonker

A Personal Glossary

The words glossed here represent my phonetic spelling of sounds as I heard them—words I was raised on in my *khutoum* (family) and community—presumably drawn from Gujarati, Kutchi, Hindi, and Swahili, and to a lesser extent, Farsi, Arabic, and Sindhi. These words are as authentic as I could make them by the rubric of memory.

agarbatti	incense
Baapre!	Oh my God! (literally: Oh Father!)
barkat	blessing
bateta champ	potato cutlets filled with ground beef blended with onions
bateta wara	deep-fried potato and meat fritters
bhajia	battered onion fritters
bhindi	okra
Bismillah	"In the name of Allah"- an invocation for beginnings and before meals
Buss!	"That's enough!"
chai	tea
chakkar	dizziness
chakra	wheel; one of seven spinning energy centers in the human body Pronounced "chuck-ruh"
chana bateta	chickpea potato stew
chash	buttermilk
chokha	rice

cobby no saag	cabbage curry
chumcha	spoon (also *chumcho* and *chumchi*)
dandiya raas	folk-dancing (in lines with sticks or clapping in concentric circles)
dhana jeera	coriander and cumin spice blend
dhokra	yellow squares of steamed savory sponge cake made from lentils
dikree	daughter
dua	prayers
gadheri	donkey
halal	allowed in Islam; usually pertains to animal slaughter and consumption
hardar	turmeric
hullo/chullo	"Come on—let's go!"
Imam	The spiritual leader of Nizari Ismaili Muslims, and a direct descendent of the Prophet Muhammad (PBUH)
jaldi	"Hurry up!"
jalebi	swirls of batter, deep-fried and soaked in sugar
jamatkhana	house of worship for Nizari Ismailies
kadhi	yogurt-based curry
kakree	cucumber
khane	short for *jamatkhana*—house of worship for Nizari Ismailies

Khuda Hafiz	"God protect you!" Often used when parting or as "goodnight"
Kiswahili	a Bantu language of the Swahili people, mostly spoken in East Africa
kitchree	a grain dish of rice and lentils cooked together until mushy
kushiali	a religious celebration observed with community festivals
kuttuck-buttuck	a colloquialism for snacking
laal	red
lilli (lili)	green
loypirni	blood-sucking
machi bhat	slow-cooked, curried fish and rice dish with whole spices and saffron
macho ngombe	fried egg (eye of cow)
maiyai	egg
masi	maternal aunt
mehman	guest
mehndi	henna body art used to create intricate designs, mostly for celebration
methi	fenugreek
Mubarak	Congratulations, felicitations, blessings
mukhi	appointed leader of the local jamat with a yearly term
muthia	a fist-shaped dumpling

Namaste	Hi/Hello (casual greeting for Indians); "The divine in me bows before the divine in you" (as adapted by Western Yogis)
nasta	snacks
ndizi	banana (Swahili)
nimuk	salt
rai	mustard seed
raita	a thin yogurt condiment blended with cucumber and mint
russ	sauce or broth
saga	relatives
samosa	triangle-shaped wrap stuffed with peas and potatoes or ground meat
soowadhana	sleeping seeds [idiomatic]; also *mukhwas*, "mouth freshener"
suferiya	saucepan
tamacho	a smack (or slap)
teepu	a drop
toppee	hat
utker	estimate
vaghar	tempered spices, fried in oil
weparis	merchants
yoga	a Vedic philosophy, popular in the West for its postures, breath-work, and mantras

Acknowledgements

Previous versions of "Fenugreek," "Spoon Mischief," and "The Side Dish" were published in the Cabrillo College *Porter Gulch Review*.

Deep gratitude to those who have nurtured my poetic voice and vision over the years:

> My colleagues at Cabrillo College, especially David Sullivan for his kind review, Barbara Bloom, Cheryl Chaffin, the late Jeff Towle, and most recently, Nikia Chaney, who, along with Ginger Galloway, midwifed this book into being.

> New friends and extraordinary poets who kindly reviewed my manuscript: Ignatius Valentine Aloysius, Carla Rachel Sameth, and Shizue Siegel.

> Canadian family and friends, beloved teachers, and collaborators over many decades—too numerous to name but each of you very much appreciated.

> Cherie for holding the phone (and me) steady and bringing rhythm to my song.

> August for recording when I spilled the chai and suggesting this title.

> Maddie for being my reader, editor, and ear. Your love for the poems and people in them has made difficult work doable.

Ongoing gratitude for the communities in which I've thrived:

- Faith of Our Foremothers—our sisterhood continues to feed me!
- Maxine Hong Kingston & The Berkeley Veterans Writing Group
- Beau Beausoleil & Al-Mutanabbi Street Starts Here
- The HIVE Poetry Collective
- Writers of Color, Santa Cruz County

A NOTE ON THE TITLE: "Spilling the chai" is a variation on the idiomatic phrase "Spill the tea," coined and popularized by African American Drag and Queer artists as "Spill the T," where T stands for truth. I am indebted to these communities for the phrase and their example.

About the Author

Geneffa Jahan is a community poet. For 20 years, she has written poems for local readings and publications in Santa Cruz, California. Her work has been published in her college's literary magazines, *Porter Gulch Review* and *Journal X*. She won their Best Poem awards in 2015 and 2021, respectively. As an organizer, she created the Salaam Initiative and Chai Society at Cabrillo College, where she has taught English since 2000. She continues to curate cultural spaces through events such as *Al-Mutanabbi Street Starts Here*. Her photo project was displayed in the traveling exhibition, *Shadow & Light*. Twice a reader for *In Celebration of the Muse*, she has helped coordinate that event for the HIVE Poetry Collective (member 2022-2024), for whom she has taped podcasts aired on KSQD's Sunday night Poetry Show. Her personal essay, "Laid to Rest," is forthcoming in *Veterans of War, Veterans of Peace, Vol. II* (2025), edited by Maxine Hong Kingston.

Born in London, England to East Indian parents from Tanzania and Uganda, Geneffa immigrated with her family to Canada at age 10, where she completed her schooling and attended university. She has lived in California since 1998. Assuming the Persian surname Jahan, for "the world," she envisions a global movement where we all heal by spilling the chai.

 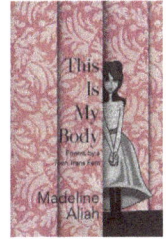  

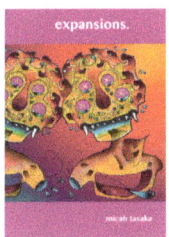   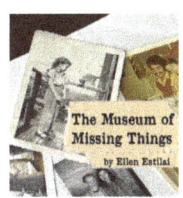

Jamii is community. At Jamii Publishing we believe that poetry is not a solitary art. Poetry is an art form that brings people together.
www.jamiipublishing.com
Jamii Publishing is a 501(c)(3) Charitable Organization

www.ingramcontent.com/pod-product-compliance
Lightning Source LLC
Chambersburg PA
CBHW071228160426
43196CB00012B/2446